DOVER BEACH

The sea is calm tonight,
The tide is full, the moon lies fair
Upon the straits; on the French coast the light
Gleams and is gone; the cliffs of England stand,
Glimm'ring and vast, out in the tranquil bay.
Come to the window, sweet is the night-air!
Only, from the long line of spray
Where the sea meets the moon-blanch'd land,
Listen! you hear the grating roar
Of pebbles which the waves draw back, and fling,
At their return, up the high strand,
Begin, and cease, and then again begin,
With tremulous cadence slow, and bring
The eternal note of sadness in.

Sophocles long ago
Heard it on the Aegean, and it brought
Into his mind the turbid ebb and flow
Of human misery; we
Find also in the sound a thought,
Hearing it by this distant northern sea.

The sea of faith
Was once, too, at the full, and round earth's shore
Lay like the folds of a bright girdle furled.
But now I only hear
Its melancholy, long, withdrawing roar,
Retreating to the breath
Of the night-wind, down the vast edges drear
And naked shingles of the world.

Ah, love, let us be true
To one another! for the world, which seems
To lie before us like a land of dreams,
So various, so beautiful, so new,
Hath really neither joy, nor love, nor light,
Nor certitude, nor peace, nor help for pain;
And we are here as on a darkling plain
Swept with confused alarms of struggle and flight,
Where ignorant armies clash by night.

—*Matthew Arnold*

Dover Beach

Matthew Arnold

Samuel Barber, Op. **3**

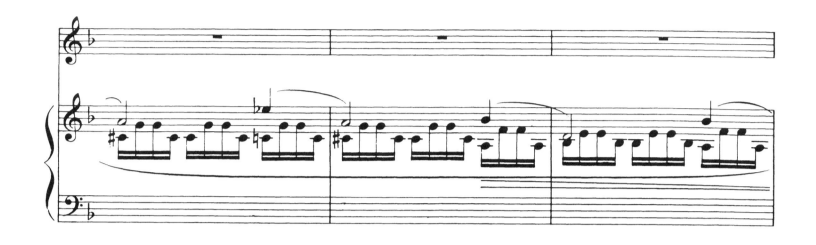

A

The tide is full, the

moon lies fair Up - on the straits; on the

sea meets the moon-blanch'd land, Lis - ten!

C

you hear the grat - ing roar Of_

peb-bles which the waves draw back, and fling, At their re-

D _poco rit._

turn, up the high strand, Be - gin, and_cease,and then_ a-gain be-

10

BARBER

DOVER BEACH

For Medium Voice and String Quartet
To the Poem of MATTHEW ARNOLD

Op. 3

for voice and piano

G. SCHIRMER, *Inc.*

DISTRIBUTED BY
HAL•LEONARD®
CORPORATION
7777 W. BLUEMOUND RD. P.O. BOX 13819 MILWAUKEE, WI 53213

love, ___ nor light, ___ Nor cer-ti-tude, nor peace, nor help for pain;

And we are

here as on a dark - ling